VOLT

Kristi Lew

Marshall Cavendish
Benchmark

New York

Other Marshall Cavendish Offices:
Marshall Cavendish International (Asia) Private Limited, 1 New Industrial Road, Singapore 536196 • Marshall Cavendish International (Thailand) Co Ltd. 253 Asoke, 12th Flr, Sukhumvit 21 Road, Klongtoey Nua, Wattana, Bangkok 10110, Thailand • Marshall Cavendish (Malaysia) Sdn Bhd, Times Subang, Lot 46, Subang Hi-Tech Industrial Park, Batu Tiga, 40000 Shah Alam, Selangor Darul Ehsan, Malaysia

Marshall Cavendish is a trademark of Times Publishing Limited

All websites were available and accurate when this book was sent to press.

Library of Congress Cataloging-in-Publication Data

Lew, Kristi.
Volt / by Kristi Lew.
p. cm. — (Green cars)
Includes bibliographical references and index.
Summary: Provides information on the electric technology used in the Volt, and discusses how the green movement is affecting the auto industry—
Provided by publisher.
ISBN 978-1-60870-013-4
1. Chevrolet automobile—Research—Juvenile literature. 2. Electric automobiles—Research—United States—Juvenile literature. 3. Experimental automobiles—Juvenile literature. I. Title.
TL215.C5L475 2011
629.22'93—dc22
2009041725

Editor: Megan Comerford
Publisher: Michelle Bisson
Art Director: Anahid Hamparian
Series Designer: Daniel Roode

Illustrations on pp. 20–21 by Alanna Ranellone

Photo research by Connie Gardner

Cover photo by Jennifer Graylook/AP Photo

The photographs in this book are used by permission and through the courtesy of: Getty Images: General Motors, 12; Alex Wong, 14; Stan Honda, 16, 26; Bill Pugliano, 24, 32, 37; Congressional Quarterly, 28; John F. Martin, 30; Getty Image News, 38, 41; Ron Kimball/www.kimballstock.com; 8; Alamy: Kristoffer Triplaar, 35; Corbis: Kim Kulish, 40.

Printed in Malaysia (T)
135642

Contents

Introduction

Most cars in the world run on gasoline, and some cars use more gas than others. Gasoline is made from petroleum, or crude oil, which is a liquid buried deep in the earth. Petroleum formed naturally from the **decomposed** and **compressed** remains of tiny **organisms** that lived millions of years ago. Humans drill deep into the earth to take the oil out.

However, the amount of oil in the world is limited. The more we take out of the ground now, the less there will be in the future, and eventually it will run out. Taking it out of the ground is expensive and damages the **environment**.

Also, when oil and the products made from oil (gasoline, engine oil, heating oil, and diesel fuel) are burned, they give off pollution in the form of gases that damage the **atmosphere**. The carbon dioxide (CO_2) that gasoline-burning engines give off is one of the major causes of **global warming**.

Carbon dioxide is a **greenhouse gas**. Like the glass panes of a greenhouse, the gas traps heat. The build-up of carbon dioxide in the atmosphere, scientists warn, is keeping Earth's heat from escaping into space. As a result, the planet is warming up.

In the United States, about 90 percent of the greenhouse gases we produce is from burning oil, gasoline, and coal. One-third of this comes from the engines that power the vehicles we use to move people and objects around. If we do not stop this global warming, life on Earth could begin to get very uncomfortable.

The problem is not just that temperatures might rise a bit. A warming atmosphere could melt the ice of the Arctic and Antarctic, raise the level of water in the seas, and change the **climate** of many places on Earth. Animals unable to adjust to the new conditions might become extinct (die out). Plants and crops might no longer be able to grow where people need them. Many islands, low-lying countries, and communities along the coasts of all the continents might disappear into the sea.

Doesn't sound so good, does it? These problems are why many people are interested in **alternative fuels** that can power our cars and other engines with less or no pollution.

Now that you know that oil is made from living things that died a long time ago, it should be no surprise that people are making oil from live plants to power their cars. This fuel, called *biodiesel*, can be made from soybean oil, canola oil, sunflowers, and other plants. One form of biodiesel is similar to the vegetable oil used for cooking. Some people gather or buy this used oil from restaurants and use it to power their cars. The engines in these cars have to be modified, or changed, in order to burn this oil correctly.

Another popular way to power cars is with batteries. Modern batteries are being made to be so powerful that some cars use them in combination with gas engines; this system is called *hybrid technology*. Hybrid cars have a gas engine and an electric motor. The electric motor usually takes over when the car runs at low speeds or when it stops.

Many auto engineers are designing electric cars that run only on batteries. Until recently, too many batteries were needed to make this an **efficient** technology. But there have been important advances in battery technology.

Another form of alternative energy for cars is the hydrogen **fuel cell**, which generates power when the hydrogen and oxygen in the fuel cell combine. If we are to start driving hydrogen-powered cars, however, hydrogen fueling stations would have to be as common along U.S. roads and highways as gas stations are today.

Oil is a limited resource, costs a lot to extract, pollutes the land, air, and water, and forces most countries to rely on the few nations that have a plentiful supply of it. If the world wants to become a cleaner, safer place, developing alternative fuels to power at least some of our vehicles is extremely important.

The Volt is a bold move. It is one of the first mass-produced vehicles to rely heavily on battery power. The Volt is even more fuel efficient than the popular Toyota Prius and Honda Insight because it only uses its gasoline engine to produce electricity when the battery charge runs out. If plug-in technology is a success, everyone might be plugging in their cars in the future!

Chapter 1

High-Voltage Ideas

The Chevrolet Volt is a hybrid car. A hybrid vehicle is one that runs on more than one power source. The Volt, for example, is equipped with an electric motor and a gasoline engine.

Many other hybrid cars also use two power sources—an electric motor that runs on electricity and a gasoline engine that burns gas. In most gas-electric hybrids, the electric motor powers the car only at low speeds. The gasoline engine takes over when the car's speed increases. When the battery charge gets low, the gasoline engine also takes over and powers the car.

◄ **The 2011 Chevrolet Volt is a good-looking car. It's also a hybrid, which means it's safer for the environment.**

The Volt works a little differently. It runs on the electric motor all the time. For part of the time, the electric motor gets power from the car's rechargeable lithium-ion batteries. These batteries are the same type of rechargeable batteries that are found in laptop computers and cell phones. When the batteries run out of electricity while the car is running, the gasoline engine in the Volt is used to make more. When the trip is over, drivers can plug the car into an electrical outlet to recharge its batteries.

WHY NOW?

In the late 1960s, the United States Congress, concerned with the air pollution caused by gasoline-powered cars, expressed an interest in electric cars. Then, in the 1970s, political tension between the United States and oil-supplying countries caused a gasoline shortage. Together, these problems resulted in an increased interest in alternative fuels among the general public as well. Suddenly, hybrid cars seemed like a really good idea.

General Motors (GM), Chevrolet's parent company, responded by building the XP-883. Revealed in the July 1969 issue of *Popular Science* magazine, the XP-883 was a plug-in hybrid vehicle that ran on electricity when it was moving at 10 miles per hour (16 km/h) or slower. But the car was never put into production.

History of Hybrids

Using electricity to run a car is not a new idea. In fact, the first electric automobile was built by Scottish inventor Robert Anderson in the 1830s. In 1891, William Morrison of Des Moines, Iowa, designed the first electric vehicle built in the United States. And in 1897, six years after Morrison unveiled his car, a fleet of electric taxicabs was introduced in New York City by the Philadelphia-based Electric Carriage and Wagon Company. At this time, many people, including inventor Thomas Edison, believed that electric cars were the future of the automobile.

At the turn of the century, Ferdinand Porsche invented the first gas-electric hybrid car. Porsche's design was similar to the design of the Volt: electric motors powered the car, and the gasoline engine was used only to generate electricity.

In the early 1900s, however, Henry Ford designed the assembly line, a new way to produce inexpensive automobiles. In 1908, the Ford Motor Company introduced the Model T, the first mass-produced gasoline-powered automobile. Now that most people could afford to buy a gasoline-powered car, electric and hybrid vehicles largely fell out of favor.

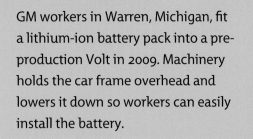

GM workers in Warren, Michigan, fit a lithium-ion battery pack into a pre-production Volt in 2009. Machinery holds the car frame overhead and lowers it down so workers can easily install the battery.

In 1996, almost thirty years after the XP-883 debuted, GM unveiled an entirely electric vehicle: the EV1. The EV1 was a very **aerodynamic** car. The year it was introduced it set the world land-speed record for an electric car at 183 miles per hour (295 kilometers/hour).

Unlike the XP-883, the EV1 did go into production. The company made and leased about 1,000 of these lightweight two-seaters. Unfortunately, the car's batteries were not able to supply enough power for the car to be driven very far. They were also expensive to make. The company did not believe that it would be able to sell enough of the cars to make a profit. Therefore, in 2003, GM announced that it would stop making the EV1.

Chapter 2
How the Volt Works

Although GM only produced the EV1 for about six years, GM officials do not consider the car a failure. Ultimately, the research and development of the EV1 helped the company develop and improve the technology, called Voltec, that powers the Volt. The EV1 was a step in the right direction, and a step toward greener cars.

The Volt can run on two different types of fuel—electricity or gasoline—so it is considered a hybrid car. Because its batteries are recharged by plugging them into a household outlet, the car is called a plug-in hybrid electric vehicle, or a PHEV. In the Volt, the gas engine functions as a support system for the electric motor.

◀ **The Volt concept car has race car attitude. Chevrolet brought the plug-in to an auto event in Washington, D.C., in 2007.**

Volt

In January 2009 the Volt's lithium-ion battery was on display at the North American International Auto Show for a press preview event.

IT'S ALL IN THE BATTERIES

The main power source in the Volt is an electric motor. People use electric motors to power all sorts of everyday appliances. Electric toothbrushes, hair dryers, blenders, vacuum cleaners, garage door openers, computers, and televisions all have electric motors. These machines do the work of pushing, pulling, cleaning, stirring, and lifting so that we do not need to do it ourselves.

The energy needed to do this work can come directly from an electrical outlet or it can be stored in batteries. In the Volt, the electric motor is powered by lithium-ion batteries until the batteries run out of charge and cannot power the car anymore. These batteries are the same type you would find in a laptop computer, a cell phone, or any number of other portable electronic devices. However, whereas the battery in a laptop computer might contain 4 to 6 lithium-ion cells, the Volt's battery pack is made up of 220 of these cells.

When the Volt is plugged into a standard 110-volt household plug, it takes about six to seven hours to completely recharge the batteries. The Volt can travel approximately 40 miles (64 km) when the batteries are completely charged.

Inside a Battery

Batteries store energy in chemical form. They have three main parts: an anode, a cathode, and an electrolyte. In a lithium-ion battery, the cathode is made of a chemical compound that contains the element lithium. The anode is made of the element carbon. The electrolyte is often made of a chemical called ether.

Electricity, or electrical energy, is created by the movement of charged particles. In a lithium-ion battery, these charged particles are free electrons and lithium ions. Atoms are electrically neutral, which means they have no electrical charge. They have the same number of positive parts, called protons, and negative parts, called electrons. Ions are made when an atom gains or loses electrons.

At the anode of a lithium-ion battery, a chemical reaction strips one electron off of a lithium atom. This reaction creates a free electron and a lithium ion. The electrons stream out of the battery's anode through wires attached to the car's electric motor. This stream of electrons is called an electrical current. The electrical energy produced by the flow of electrons runs the motor.

As the flow of electrons leaves the battery, the positive lithium ions move from the anode to the cathode. To recharge the battery, the car is plugged into an electrical socket overnight. Now electrons from the plug flow into the battery and the lithium ions move the opposite way—from the cathode to the anode. The battery is recharged and ready to produce electricity again.

GOING THE DISTANCE

But what happens if you want to go farther than 40 miles (64 km)? This is where the Volt's gasoline engine comes into play. This engine does not actually power the car, as it does in regular cars and in hybrids like the Prius and Insight. Instead, it is hooked up to a machine called a generator.

An electric generator is a device that creates a stream of charged particles by moving a **conductor**, such as a copper bar or wire, through a magnetic field. In the Volt the gas engine is hooked up to a generator, which is connected to the electric motor. The engine enables the generator to produce a flow of charged particles, which power the electric motor so that a person can drive the car when the batteries have run out of charge.

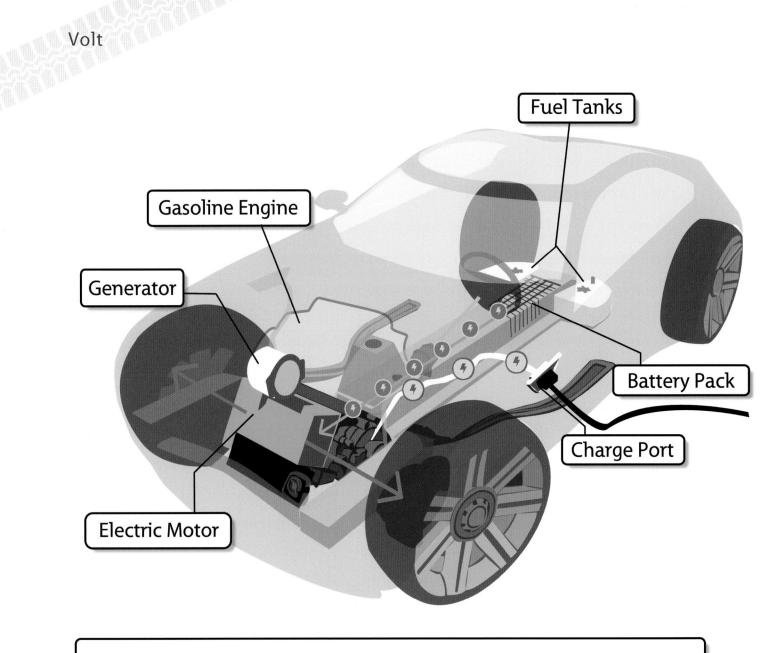

Fuel Tanks

Gasoline Engine

Generator

Battery Pack

Electric Motor

Charge Port

Running on Electric Power

⚡ Electrical charge is stored in the battery

⚡ The battery powers the motor

— The motor powers the car so a person can drive it

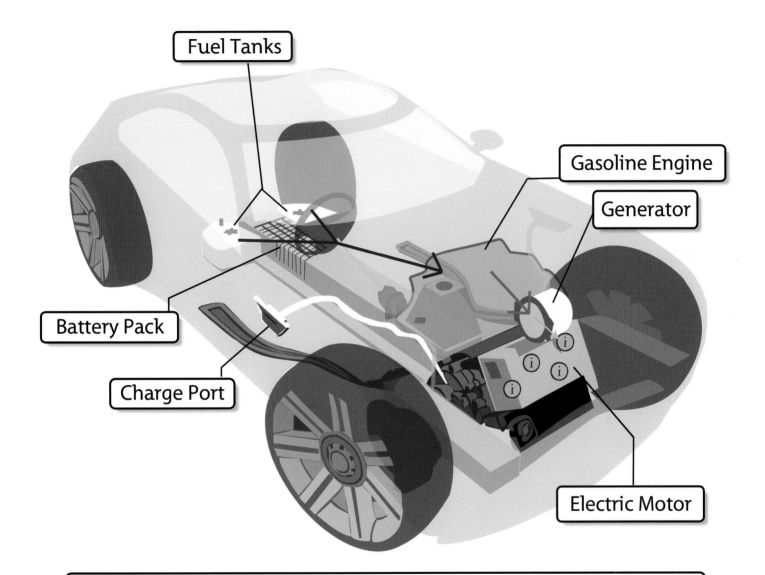

Fuel Tanks

Gasoline Engine

Generator

Battery Pack

Charge Port

Electric Motor

Running on Hybrid Power

— The fuel tanks hold gasoline to fuel the engine

— The engine powers the generator

ⓘ Charged particles from the generator power the electric motor

Having a generator on board makes it possible for the Volt to travel more than 40 miles (64 km). It extends the car's range. With completely charged batteries and a tank full of gasoline, the car can travel for more than 600 miles (966 km). If you need to go farther than 600 miles (966 km), a quick stop at a gas station—or hooking up to an outlet for several hours—will keep the car going.

POWER UP!

The generator is not the only part of the Volt that can make electricity. The brakes help, too.

When a driver steps on the brakes in a traditional car, a brake pad rubs against the rotor, a disk connected to the car's wheels. The **friction** created by this pressure slows the car down. In the process, the kinetic energy that is moving the car forward is converted into heat energy. This heat energy is lost into the air around the car.

That's not how things work in the Volt. When a driver steps on the brakes in a Volt, an onboard computer, called the controller, reverses the direction of the electric current in the motor. This direction change causes the wheels to slow down. But it also does something else: it generates electricity. This electricity is captured and is used to recharge the car's batteries. This type of braking system is called regenerative braking.

The controller not only manages electricity created by the braking system. It has many other functions, too. For example, the controller varies the amount of electricity supplied to the electric motor based on the position of the car's accelerator. This determines the car's speed.

If the driver wants to move slowly and lightly pushes the accelerator pedal, the motor only gets a little bit of energy. If the driver wants to move quickly—while driving on a highway, for example—and pushes the accelerator pedal closer to the floor, the controller allows more electricity to flow into the motor so that the car has more power to go fast.

The controller also switches on the gasoline-powered generator when the batteries are running low on electricity. The driver doesn't have to worry about monitoring the battery charge. As long as there is gas in the tank, the controller will automatically adjust to provide power from the generator to the motor so that the car keeps running when the batteries are out of charge.

Chapter 3

Unveiling the Volt

The first version of the Volt, called a **concept car**, was introduced at the 2007 North American International Auto Show. Concept cars are often brought to auto shows so people can see what car companies are working on for the future. The concept Volt had a different look from the 2011 model that Chevrolet plans to sell to the public. Cars that are sold to consumers are called production models.

◄ **Jennifer Granholm, the governor of Michigan, got to drive a Volt past GM employees to a stage for a press conference in December 2009.**

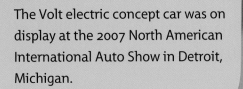

The Volt electric concept car was on display at the 2007 North American International Auto Show in Detroit, Michigan.

VISION OF THE VOLT

When GM unveiled the first Volt in 2007, the car had an angular body. However, the boxy shape was not very efficient. It takes a lot of power to push a square shape through the air. The air pushes against the car, creating resistance. This air resistance is called drag.

To overcome the drag, a car must use more power. In a gas-powered car, using more power means using more gas. When the car runs on batteries, as the Volt does, the need for more power means the batteries are drained quicker. Chevrolet engineers found that drag caused the generator in the concept Volt to take over sooner to produce more electrical energy. Both of these situations caused the generator to burn more gas.

In order to get better gas mileage and a 40-mile (64-km) range on a single battery charge, the shape of the car needed to be more rounded. A curvier shape is more aerodynamic. It reduces the drag on the car so that it moves through the air more easily. This makes the car more energy efficient. Increased efficiency allows the Volt to be driven longer without having to switch over to the generator or recharge the batteries. This means a greener car.

Chevrolet engineers went back to the drawing board to redesign the body of the Volt. The car-buying public got its first peek at the sleeker production model of the Volt in September 2008.

GM had a cutaway frame of the Volt concept car at the Washington Auto Show. Visitors could see the battery, engine, motor, and other parts of the hybrid system.

PLUG IT IN!

The Volt is not the only extended-range vehicle that GM makes. The same year that the car company unveiled the concept car for the Volt, it also introduced the Opel Flextreme at the International Motor Show in Frankfurt, Germany. The technology in the Flextreme is very similar to that in the Volt.

The main differences are that the Flextreme generator runs on diesel or biodiesel fuel rather than gasoline, and it is charged using a 220-volt electrical supply instead of a 110-volt outlet. The reason for these differences is that GM plans to sell the Flextreme in Europe instead of in the United States. Diesel fuel is much more common in Europe than it is in America. Also, European households are wired with 220-volt electrical plugs instead of the 110-volt plugs that are more common in the United States.

Fun Facts

The Volt was a high-priority project for GM. The company assigned more than two hundred engineers and fifty designers to work on the Volt—and just the Volt. An additional four hundred people were enlisted to develop and perfect the car's subsystems and electrical components. That's more that 650 men and women working on one car!

Cadillac, a car brand produced by GM, also has an electric car in the works. The Converj was part of an event at the 2009 North American International Auto Show in Detroit, Michigan.

In 2009 GM unveiled the Opel Ampera, another plug-in hybrid for the European market. Unlike the Flextreme, however, the Ampera has a gasoline-driven generator just like the Volt does.

That same year the Cadillac Converj made its first appearance at the Detroit Auto Show. The Converj is a luxury model with Voltec, the same technology as the Volt. GM hopes to develop the Converj for the U.S. marketplace by 2013.

GM is not the only car company releasing plug-in hybrids. Fisker, a relatively new American carmaker, introduced the Karma at the 2008 International Auto Show in Detroit. Like the Volt, the Karma runs on lithium-ion batteries for the first 40 or 50 miles (64 or 80 km). Then a gasoline generator takes over to power the car.

One major difference between the Karma and the Volt is that some of the electricity produced by the Karma's generator is used to recharge the car's batteries. In the Volt, the electricity produced by the generator is used only to power the car. Another difference is that Fisker's four-door luxury sports car is about twice the price of the Volt. The company plans to deliver the first Karma hybrids to select car dealerships in late 2010.

Chrysler, Mazda, and Mitsubishi have plug-in hybrids either in development or scheduled for release in the United States soon, too. Toyota has announced plans to launch a plug-in version of the popular Prius in 2011 as well.

Chapter 4

The Future Is Electrifying!

Chevrolet plans to have the newest version of the Volt ready for people to buy by the end of 2010. This plan depends on successful testing of the car's lithium-ion battery packs. These batteries have never been used in a car before.

In order for the car to be ready for the marketplace, the batteries must meet quality, performance, and safety standards. For example, the batteries must pass quality tests to make sure that they do not lose power too quickly.

◀ **The Volt was the subject of a press conference in August 2009. GM executives announced that the Volt gets an estimated 230 miles per gallon (98 km/l).**

Performance tests ensure the batteries are able to supply enough power to run the car under a variety of driving conditions. Safety standards guarantee that the batteries work without catching on fire or failing in some other way that could harm people. If the batteries can pass all the tests and meet the standards, the Volt should be on the market as scheduled.

WHY BUY A PLUG-IN HYBRID?

Owning a plug-in, like the Volt, could potentially save people a lot of money. In preliminary tests, GM reports that the Volt can get about 230 miles per gallon (98 kilometers per liter) driving around town. This reported gas mileage is possible because the car uses no gasoline at all for any trip that is 40 miles (64 km) or shorter. For many people, trips to and from work, school, or the store are shorter than 40 miles (64 km).

Just because it does not always use gasoline does not mean that the Volt is free to operate, however. To charge the car's batteries, it must be plugged into an electrical outlet. This would most likely increase the driver's electric bill. However, electricity is still cheaper than gasoline, and it's even less expensive in the middle of the night, which is a convenient time for most people to charge their plug-in vehicles.

The Volt's charging port is located in front of the driver's-side door.

Fun Facts

If the electricity used to charge the batteries in a plug-in hybrid comes from nuclear or alternative energy sources and the generator engine is modified to run on biodiesel, the only petroleum product the car would need would be engine oil.

In addition, if a trip is longer than 40 miles (64 km), gasoline will have to be bought as well. However, depending on a person's driving needs, owning a plug-in hybrid has the possibility of being less expensive than owning a traditional car.

Plug-in hybrids also have the potential to reduce the amount of pollution in the air. As long as the Volt is being operated by the electric motor, it does not release any waste chemicals, called emissions, from its tailpipe. In this purely electric state, the Volt produces no pollution. A car that does not give off waste chemicals as a result of its onboard power system is called a zero-emission vehicle.

However, none of the plug-in hybrid vehicles, including the Volt, are completely fossil-fuel free. Even if an owner only drives the Volt less then 40 miles (64 km) a day, the car still needs to be plugged into a house-

The Volt took center stage at General Motors' 100th anniversary celebration in 2008.

Chief Engineer of the Volt, Andrew Farah, gets behind the wheel of the first Volt in June 2009.

hold socket to be recharged. The electricity supplied to most households by electric power plants across the United States is produced by burning coal. Like gasoline, coal is a fossil fuel, and when it is burned carbon dioxide is released into the air.

Power plants around the country are in the process of developing newer, cleaner technology that should reduce their emissions in the future. In addition, some areas of the country supplement the electricity produced by power plants with electricity made by alternative energy sources, such as solar, wind, and water power.

Nuclear power is another way to get electricity without burning fossil fuels. If it is possible for a Volt owner to get electricity from only these sources, the Volt could be a zero-emission, practically fossil-fuel-free car.

Vital Stats

1996 EV1

Electric Motor: 137 hp

Gasoline Engine: none

Top Speed: 80 mph (129 km/h)

0–60 mph (0–97 km/h): 8–9 seconds

Curb Weight: 3,084 lbs (1,399 kg)

Battery life: estimated 60–90 miles (97–145 km)

2011 VOLT

Electric Motor: 150 hp

Gasoline Engine: 4-cylinder, 1.4-liter engine with a 12-gallon (54.4-liter) gas tank

Top Speed: 100 mph (161 km/h)

0–60 mph (0–97 km/h): 8–8.5 seconds

Curb Weight: 3,500 lbs (1,588 kg)

Fuel Efficiency: 230 mpg (98 km/l)

Battery life: 40 miles (64 km)

Glossary

aerodynamic Shaped to reduce drag.

alternative fuels Substances, other than gasoline and other petroleum products, that can be used to power engines.

anode The negative electrode of a battery.

atmosphere The air surrounding Earth.

cathode The positive electrode of a battery.

climate The average weather of a place over many years

compressed Squeezed together; in the case of the life-forms that became oil, they were pressed together over millions of years by layers of rock and soil.

concept car The first version of a new car.

conductor An object that an electrical current can easily flow through.

decomposed Broken down into parts or basic elements; when plants or animals die, because of time, weather, and the action of insects and bacteria, they are broken down.

efficient To function without much waste or unnecessary effort.

electrolyte A substance through which ions can move.

electrons	Negatively charged particles that move around an atom's nucleus.
environment	The rock, soil, air, and water that sustains all life, as well as the life-forms they sustain.
friction	The force, in the form of heat, that is generated when two solid objects rub against each other.
fuel cell	A device that changes a chemical fuel, such as hydrogen, into electrical energy, which can power a vehicle.
global warming	An increase in Earth's average yearly temperature, believed to be caused by pollution and that results in climate changes.
greenhouse gas	A gas, such as carbon dioxide, that contributes to global warming.
ions	Charged particles created when an atom loses or gains electrons.
organisms	Living things.
protons	Positively charged particles found in an atom's nucleus.

Further Information

BOOKS

Bearce, Stephanie. *Tell Your Parents All about Electric and Hybrid Cars.* Hockessin, DE: Mitchell Lane Publishers, 2009.

Famighetti, Robert. *How Do Hybrid Cars Work?* Science in the Real World. New York: Chelsea House, 2009.

Flaherty, Michael. *Electricity & Batteries. Science Factory.* New York: PowerKids Press, 2008.

Rau, Dana Meachen. *Electricity and Magnetism. Real World Science.* Ann Arbor, MI: Cherry Lake Publishing, 2009.

Solway, Andrew. *Generating and Using Electricity. Why Science Matters.* Chicago, IL: Heinemann Library, 2009.

WEBSITES

Chevrolet.com, the official website of the Volt, provides information on the technology used in the Volt, features a photo gallery, and has a place to post questions of your own.
www.chevrolet.com/pages/open/default/future/volt.do

EEK! Environmental Education for Kids, and electronic magazine about the environment and environmental issues produced by the Wisconsin Department of Natural Resources for students in grades 4 to 8.
www.dnr.state.wi.us/org/caer/ce/eek/earth/index.htm

Energy Kids, a website run by the Energy Information Administration, provides information about energy use in the United States.
http://tonto.eia.doe.gov/kids/

Energy Quest is the California Energy Commission's guide to alternative fuel vehicles. There is information on cars that run on gasoline, hydrogen, electricity, and biodiesel, as well as links to sources with more information.
www.energyquest.ca.gov/transportation/

Index

The page numbers in **boldface** are photographs, illustrations, or diagrams.

Index

About the Author

Kristi Lew is the author of more than two dozen science books for teachers and young people. Fascinated with science from a young age, she studied biochemistry and genetics in college. Before she started writing full-time, she worked in genetics laboratories for more than ten years and taught high school science. When she's not writing, she enjoys sailing with her husband aboard their small sailboat, *Proton*. She writes, lives, and sails in St. Petersburg, Florida.